The Abandoned Eye

Poems by
J. P. Dancing Bear

FutureCycle Press

Mineral Bluff, Georgia

Published by FutureCycle Press
Mineral Bluff, Georgia, USA

ISBN 978-1-938853-09-8

Contents

For Rain

The Invitation

There was no mercy in the careful curls of your cursive.
Still, I came. I jumped into the crude hole you left
in the earth and planted myself

a field of grass and corn. Now, I have become
the queen of locusts. My subjects bow
as best they can in their tiny bodies built

for leaping and eating. They taught me voracity
and I taught them never to trust an invitation—
most are traps. Even their cricket cousins

in cages of gold sing of solitude—beautifully,
so their jailers say. Rubbing their legs together
in a gospel about freedom and the Moses

of the crickets. Every day I tell the locusts
they are free to fly away. I stand here in this distant place,
tending my crop and my subjects. I read to them
the dark and folded words of your invitation.

Genesis in Retrograde

We started in our paper boats,
ambitious as maps.
We were minutes and hours,
our longitudes spreading tendrils
beyond the boundaries of the key.
We saw the world as something
waiting for us,
but that was just our expectations
pinpointing to particular coordinates.
We reduced the planet
to a scaled globe
smaller than a human heart.

Magpie in My Own Image

I built another bird with cages within—
some level of amusement—
a private glow.

These cold days and the magpie catches my eye still.
Marvel of my creation—I can hear its hinges creak,
which the unobservant mistake
for a caw.

I watch it scavenge—a consequence
of careless programming—
too busily loving my tinker-hands
ticking the gears and springs
into place.

Someone once said, *god loves a flywheel*,
and that is the only god I can believe in.
Loud cries for grease—a prayer
unless the voice is so lovely in song
that even the sweet-whispered snow,
the long-breathed whistle of grasswinds
is no competition for the divinity of an ear

—though I have it to spare, I cannot bear oil.

The Mirrored Narcissus

"I can barely touch my own self—
how can I touch someone else?"
                              —David Bryne

We watched him drop his face
to the water—a statue
of his former life. *The water*
makes everything look better,
and then he was gone again.
Touching his reflection as though
something would feel it back.

He may have fallen
asleep.

We laughed and mused his issues while,
over square fields, scattering us
as wildling flower seeds
of the unshared visions of ourselves.

Who last reached for his shoulder?
All this false concern!—was it really
jealousy? Did he become a golden idol
in the sunset? We bloomed clinical labels
as though we knew explanations,
as though we knew *him*.

In that stretch of shadows
the feral dogs turned to rocks.
Small landmarks along the undiscovered
borders.
              He might have been
dreaming of a storm strong enough
to cleanse the imprints.

Someone, like one of us, grinded
a worry stone about the delicate cycle
of self-esteem; at the edge of obsession
everything blurred into impressions

                                        ...into art.

He made one last attempt to speak:
I was naked once—
long before my own statue
flowered its first crack.

A woman in our crowd turned
to plaster; near her a man's shadow
painted itself into the rut of a road.
I turned my eyes to the rest
and we moved on together,
forgetting their names.

Legitimacy Is So Chummy

First thing is: everyone presses the room.
To handshake the perimeter
like a grass snake:
the clammy waiting to get their chance at you.
Go on, handyswipe boy. Give them a little wink.
Listen: you tell them what they want.
You get it and you are kind.
Maybe everyone wins the big contract.
Maybe we could all be stockholders.
What do you say? Calluses only show
on the outside. You're one
of those guys, never built a muscle
but pillowy hands.
Say, *Hello.*
Say, *let's do business.*
I've always loved you
like a wallet, you know.

Deadline World

This way every minute is the last.
I jammed my thumb shoving paper in
the printer, pressed the key,
let it fly with one eye on the ticking time.
Someone quotes the love of adrenaline,
but I don't know—love, proper love, takes
time. Now a voice over
the cube wall says, *better to have loved
and lost than never to have...* the loser.
I overhear the quote about wages
not keeping up with the cost of living,
and then I cannot remember
what milk tastes like.
I think it must be thick and flabby
and it might be sweet, because...
why else?
Someone's radio reports
that siphoning from tanks
and driving away without paying
at the pump has increased
at an alarming rate.
Alarm bells—I think it all began there
with dual-function, the alarm bell that marked
panic and signaled the next class all in one.
I had to run the length of the school
not to be tardy. I had all the state-issued books
on my back. Out of breath and sliding
into a chair at the bell.
The clock resets itself every hour,
you know. Just now, I'm three minutes
into the next deadline.

Hold

She believed in the power of positive thinking, hence the blindfold. Hungry as she was, she performed her nightly ritual starting with setting the table. Plate and utensils resting on the flat table adorned with the cruelties of wax fruit. An empty jug of wine—its green glass dinged by dust. She puts on her black dress, the one saved for special occasions, brushes her hair and slips black fabric over her eyes, tying it behind her head. She sits at the table, lifts the knife and the fork, the prongs sliding, puncturing the air above the plate. Then the blade slices the emptiness. The shadows on the surface of the colored ceramic glaze tell their own stories of uselessness and need. She raises the silver to her mouth and makes the motions of chewing. The bottle watches with envy, desiring lips for the breath of its own tune of vacancy. She believes in small prayers whispered throughout the day. She stirs her mind against obvious negativities, even as the smell of someone else's dinner wafts into the room.

Knot

Even as the last red tongues of our tree
cling to a colder life, I see your bones
among the naked branches
where even my smallest prayer
falls to mulch.
I entwine my limbs into silent knots
with yours, and think not of death,
but what I can remember
of your body—its shape and fragrance,
the hunger it generates
within me. And yes,
my tears have watered this tree,
for what else is there
but to nurture what memory provides.

Personal

for Jason Bredle

O Cello Head, sing me a song of Yo-Yo Ma
and the tragedy of papier-mâché. Every
            Sunday, Sunday, Sunday
news of the Auto-Casa in E-flat major.
God came to you in a classified ad.
God says, *must love sunrises, must*
love ohio tire fires, must love '50s
auto fins. God is a hopeful romantic
            in a valentine-red Cadillac
with a cardiac condition for smoke
and fireballs. You have seen god on
the interstate. Hair almost Medusan
with the top down. He hits the horn
every time he sees the bumper sticker
"honk if you love god"—God loves god—
            you know it's true.
All the dogs are barking—you know God
loves Dog too. O Cello Head, you are
            finding poems in the classifieds.

Martha's House of Cards

let's not talk about how you cheated: that bending Queen of Hearts: on her third floor balcony: or how you finally chewed your pencil to a nub: just as your mother once predicted: let's not talk about the other faces: locked in the chambers of your house: you said: *we picked our pleasures*: and it's true: something else was bending: the books began to warp in the ocean air: your feelings becoming suits: bludgeoning clubs: cutting spades: the sharp edges of diamonds: the lonely curves and point of a heart

I, Michigan

Work whistle: limbs rising but tingle half asleep.
Tornado warnings in the breezes, sparrows quiet,
the work-damned shuffle onto rumble buses
with busted mufflers—they dart traffic like grotesque
ambulances on our way to somewhere tragic, somewhere
automatic, without any witnesses. We mull
around other bodies like crows, picking almost
    pneumatically,
pretending our boundaries, the false hope of space,
somnambulant, this lever up, pull and push away, next
dreary widget. Is this what Hell is? Could it be this easy?
As mundane a haze, still as fog, systematic as robots?
Free coffee and doughnuts in the breakroom—15 minutes
then back. Back down to the clean concrete floors.
Someone etched *I Love You* on a part—best report it to
    Quality Control.

Piano from Scratch

for Kemel Zaldivar

Because you love the music of birds, I built
a piano that cannot translate chirps very well.
In my effort to perfect its translations, I've turned
the legs to curl inward and upward. I've added
abstract sculptures in hopes of making a better
sound—I designed a building where sound might
escape more pleasantly; but I assure you
it was not my main priority. I studied histories,
birds, men, and the sea. All of it cycloning into
the piano. And then I studied the instrument,
the wood, the composition of materials before
I sketched it. You have to understand the whale
if you want to get the acoustics right. You need to
measure the empty heart, if only to perfect the pitch.

Tempt

I was afraid of their tempting rain
and the lusting flowers in my heart.

I felt an ass most of my life under their craft,
always staring at the wrong things—lumps

in my throat, the backs of my hands beginning
to spot with age.

They pulled out of me a spirit long since
absent. Ghosts haunting a younger night,

desirous, restless, burning with a passion-
fire I have learned to dowse.

I said the word *love*, over again, *love*,
as though it was a turret I called home.

I covered my head, my eyes, ducked low,
afraid of the shapes clouds might become.

Island

perhaps the body drifts: the bed edges closer to the water: the towering flower growing from the true center of the mattress: is your personal tree of knowledge: as you curl yourself to sleep around its trunk: you watch the stars reflected from the surface of the still sea: small fish mocking the moon's silvery shocked expression: coming up close enough to scoop with your hand: you fantasize umbrellas: but not as some droll coverage: more as sails to catch wind: pull this knuckle of land in a direction: you feel the clouds slipping through you: as though you are some ghost: a shipwrecked sole survivor: having spent this lifetime: on a bedrock: and a salvaged bed: each light on the horizon: a hopeful bonfire: blinking a billion years ago

Magic, Isn't It

You, the imp among the light sockets.
All block-eyed and torquing a spell
of ozone. Scroll of carpet rot...
an *I curse thee...* Love as eye
of newt or bat wing—or wiggly thing
mixed into the bigger cauldron.
O black cat, O matted wanderer,
evil never walks into a room
but is waiting for the interviewer
to ask him the question he's always wanted.
There is so much fading
to black. God rolled a twenty-sided dice
once—then all hell broke loose.
You were thinking of going back to sawing
young assistants in half—
not nearly the sticky mess on your karma—
it's less trouble, really, and the pay's much better.

A Little Night Music

she says *that damn sunflower is such an insufferable tune*: it
lets itself into the house: in the middle of the night: searching
for the sun: annoyed by the empty dish of a moon: it creaks
the stairs: pulls open the doors: a real poltergeist: then she
droops against the frame: her shadow a silent twin who has
that look of a girl in a window who cannot go out and play:
you feel the chill of the petaled presence: static electricity
enough to make your seed-black hair stand on end: snake
wildly: like ribbons coming undone in the wind: you can feel
the broken stalk of the thing: you hear its siren voice: calling
everyone awake: the cracking of seeds on the sanguine
carpet: echoing down the hall: your sister she says *that damn
sunflower*...: as she grips a torn petal: you can make out the
body of it at the top of the stairs: the abandoned eye: search-
ing for its god: you are remembering a passage from a movie:
or a book: or play: where the sunflower is a symbol for life
and death: you want to cradle it in your arms: hold onto the
last moments of the old day: not crying: but humming some-
thing nearly forgotten: some rhyme from younger days

El Amante

you say: *love is the flowers of my mouth*: and out spill color:
petals: leaves: roots: an early spring: enough that I call you
Green Tongue: your irises: are irises: that rise up to the
roiling dark skies: your hands bleed beautifully: the field: here
I pick the strawberry of your heart: and dream your body in
dark broad leaves: you spread your arms: become the field:
while I sway: a daisy

A Blue Mountain at Sunset

you feel like half a shroud: someone who is far too intimate
with clouds: they ghost through you: into blue: here where
the air thins: where there is more stone than mountain top:
you say there are no words for love: but forty-three words for
rust: dozens for various kinds of shadow: those that darken
the body: others that turn granite to indigo: so stars can find
their way back into the sky: there are the words like names
for the magnitude of lightning strikes: a thought fires and zig-
zags along its synapse path: I call your name: it is the only
word I have: for such feelings

Aubade with Red-Tailed Hawk

Within my shirt
the last reeds of
hay whistle
the saddest song.
Splintered wood—
my crucifixion bones.
The cloth faded
as an autumn day.
A hawk for a head
still vowing to keep
vigil over the field
now gone to stubble.
The moths are home
within these tatters
and threadbare
appearances.
Yes, I remember
everything, as
though it was just in
the previous season.

Be That Releasable

Last week my heart was a whale—well,
it was something with a blowhole,
disappearing, going deep into the belly
of the Pacific. Love, last week
as I walked the shoreline
searching for spouts,
I saw 30 dead bees washed up.
What brought them to the ocean?—
There are no flowers on the beach.
Einstein (well, the voice I've assigned him)
whispered, "Once they've gone, we go."
Can you think of the Earth invested?
Or the bees? There is such static in the air
when I think of my heart as a cell-phone
tower, transmitting insecticide,
the wrong math
to the little quantum minds of pollen-
ation. Queen bee, your hive
is not a whale in the sea.
Everything hangs,
and it doesn't matter that we've worked
the maxim of release exactly.

Driven

I carry my visions where
they cannot buck and rear
in the unfurling landscape.
Here in my corral heart
I am anxious
to unhinge the gate.

My visions gallop with me.
Even in this tiny vessel
they lean over the prow
breathing in the night
until the stars form new
constellations around their heads.

In a world of hulls
my visions are rising
hooves that extend beyond
the pen of my body
and carry me
into unknown light.

Reflection in a Fishbowl

Goldfish float gradually around my head
as though I were an ornament
placed in the center of their world:
castle, sunken ship, the helmeted diver.

They are reminders of a lost sea—
fallen from maps, not the end of the world
where continents go to die,
but more like leaves over an edge.

My thoughts are bubble-eyed,
butterfly-winged, marigold ghosts
gliding along the curved proximity
of my *little* world.

This fishbowl fluidity is not lost on me
as they pass through the sea-grass
of my hair. They fantail, they celestial eye,
they ryukin and adorn my face.

How often have I looked upon a body
of water and filled it with an idea
of loneliness when below the surface
life teamed.

We Form a Line

I.

Each measured step forward
is met with the crunch of graveled stars.

Our bodies and the shadows of our bodies
build our own long staircase
to solve our loneliness.

We walk a deliberate pace
with our heads bent slightly forward—
one eye on the promised heaven-light,
one eye on the flicker-dance of flame—
crimson candles to match our robes,
bright enough to make a garland
of dull suns on the wall

—another vow as a reminder of vows.

II.

Sometimes I get lost
in my thoughts while I stare
at the cast stardust
we stride upon.

Each step is a whisper
among the exploded galaxies.

III.

When my lips move,
I love you like a shroud
slips out like a dove from my eaves.

Now I am sorrowful
and aware of myself
beneath the wrappings of traditions,
in love
with another shroud
who has never turned to look
back.

IV.

Behind me I feel all the love
in my life building
and unseen
as though I were Orpheus
holding onto a vow
against certainty
but still silently climbing
the long steps
out of darkness.

I needed to speak,
to whisper those words
against the building line
of love.

V.

I want to lessen my devotion
to the candle and the perfection
of measured counts, rhythms
and vows, reach
one hand forward from beneath
these robes
and touch the flow

and ripple
of her shroud.

Does she not also
feel the weight
of a line?

VI.

Would we not spiral arm
and arm together?—

become a dance.

Would our voices break
into dust and gravel?—

become a gorgeous
event.

VII.

This deliberate pace—
each step in our stairway
a year passing under our feet.

The measure of our bodies,
our candles, our flames

deliberately paced
forward to a promise

of something better than
the visible starry heaven—

a step closer to that
blinding light of belief.

Nocturne

I am stolen horses for you.
My body no more
than a wooden dingy
and dropped lines.
Still I breathe out
planets and stars for you;
all the dust in a god's eye.
My hair is the streaks
of comets and meteors.
My bones fill with crickets
and frog music.
As the world turns its
shoulder to the sun
I bend into the boat
of this journey.
I am in a night
created for you.

Urge Evolution

First it's some guy with hair everywhere,
out pounding the sticks and stones
for a meal. He finds like minds,
he feels a stirring in those hairier places.
Next there's a stadium full of people
chanting, *BEL-LY, BEL-LY, BEL-LY!*
And it doesn't matter what inning
it is when Hunger comes to the plate.
They are all here to watch the table set;
they want to feast and drink and see
with their reptilian pocket drives.
The big celebration, the after party,
the drunken glow, the *Homo erectus* jet set,
rub the elbows and the gums—
satiated quickly, before urge sparks again.

Unraveling Trees

the years offer themselves as concentric rings
each cycle internalized, a living record

ripple of circles and vibrations
ripple of mouths and grass

much of landscape patterns away
from your open branches

your trunk electric and alive
with each gust a sough of leaves

branches creak—
the teaching of crickets begins

more and more the insects reach out
to message the remaining trees

your face is layer upon layer
of leaves and a nest of bees

feel the clusters of nuts
buried deep within your buds

even now you begin to

tell the squirrels to dig a little deeper
forget a little more

into what soil remains
to fight against

the undeniable color of concrete
weighing down the world

it's all about containment and control
walls within walls, dear prisoner

like layers or rings
built up over years of scarring

the sun tumbles over the moon
again and again
until a season is renewed

over time it becomes so much
dressing and undressing

sometimes you are unsure
whether it is the moment
of stripping down
or building green

a twilight settles into your body

and the other trees offer no hints
no tells

the world offers its chill air
and breeze

the sky full of rain that signals neither
one nor the other direction

go ahead and ravel or unravel
it will not change a single thing on this planet

[We lived on the crest of a wave]

We lived on the crest of a wave
so quiet through our lives
that we thought it was made of ice
left over from another age.

The bare arms of trees rose
to meet the distant sun
like a prayer whispered
by the wind over frost.

Snow fell on the small shrine
for those creatures
often overlooked
in our newfound modernity.

Icicles on the lip
of the wave gave
the appearance of fangs
and still we did not notice

a single drop of thaw.

The Listening Post

after an art installation by Mark Hansen & Ben Rubin

what if god: is the sound of our voices: combined: all the things we've ever said: or scrawled: typed out in the witching hours of our lives: repeated back to us: all at once: until we are a music: a continuum: wrapping: ribboning around: the curve of space: stretching across the universe: time to listen to the sung word: coming back through us: *hello*

Frogpond

You are the shape of death kneeling among the lily pads.
The laid-out, prepared bodies not sleeping.
The crucifix was your own, borrowed, put to use here...
splayed to look like a sacrifice, upright, a punishment,
    a lesson plan, a warning.
It is a mythic lie to think of the carcasses as reclined,
    relaxing, sleeping on their lily beds.
It is as if your pink skin is a poison
and you've cleared this pond by diving in. Something you
are known for—some might even call it a *signature move*.
                                    Even now,
you are scheming in concrete. You see the little dead
harbingers cleared away for a kiddy pool.
You close your ears and shout *la-la-la* should anyone
accuse you of being an animal, an introduced species,
that enters like a bullet wound. The sky is a harsh season—
unnatural rain falls as a condemnation. Wading further in,
the browning leaves and dying fish in your wake, you say
it's water off your back, though no duck will land here.

Persephone: Cream, Cherries, and the Diagramed Heart

today I have read up on the heart: diagramed in blue veins:
red arteries: sliced to show the chambers: the valves: doors
that open and close: sure as a season: what do you know:
eating pairs of cherries: red as muscles in an anatomy book:
wondering if he knows what you feel: you sit here patient as
a blue pitcher of cream: complimenting tea cups: that look
like you and him: here in a twilight kitchen: you read the
crimson history of the underworld: chambered: half punish-
ment: half honored dead: sit sipping your clouding tea: now
cold to your lips: you run a finger tracing veins: the highways
to and from the diagramed heart: nearly the map of Hades:
itself: with the first rustle of his awakening: you prepare: the
breakfast table: greet him in a black dress: though you wish it
the color of sky

Quadruple Life

I was out there with my quadruple lives,
trying to keep them straight.
Someone says *who is that guy*
and even I turn to look at one
of my selves'
unrecognizable blue eyes—
the shade of sky in front
of a bank of gray.

In these candle-scorched days,
only the rich get their one life
with the romance of a second
being a mysterious adventure.

My second fell in love
with someone's third
but none of our others could
agree to the union—

churches of objectors
raising their fists
while Jesus perched and sighed;
his first, third, and fourth lives
completely unknown.

Only the famous Jesus
still hangs on,
catching no moss
in the steepled hands
of alternative lives

pressed together
in single dwelling houses.

The Turning

I see the whalebone sky
through the fog of my glass coffin

water falls asleep in my hand
a silversmith dripping a ticking

clock of my days—I have a recurring dream
of white fire girls trapped in icebergs

of the arctic—holding their breaths
against the warming

each a siren warning of a certain doom
each locked within a case

fragile as an eagle's egg
I go on envisioning fish

drifting around the frozen reef
of my aquarium

of the quick damage
and the slow healing of an age

a geologic period
a fossil in the Himalayas

currents fishtail through
my calcium bars

and I hear the song of snow
spindrifting off the highest peaks

my sleep remains a starless one
I shall attempt no further footfall

—everyone has their own stories
of how god loved them once

before turning away

Landscape without Crossing Signal

A herd of trains steaming the divided prairie
where last dusk I saw the shadowing horse gallop
headlong into the oncoming twilight—its breath
clouding like an engine, and in that gloom the animal
looked made of iron. My head heavy with wild
reenactments of metaphorical history and impending
collision. How the stallion streamlined its body
to an aerodynamic grace, maneless, ears like the slicing
fins of cars. The train with its forward lamp a beacon
as the transforming hooves kicked plumes

that drifted into the consuming grass. Muscles rippled
in the darkening mist until the outline of the equine
was overtaken. As though all the creatures that had
evolved over the tracked time had ceased to produce
a single horse. The train gained in size; its rumble became
more deafening than could be absorbed by prairie roots.
Each face in the lighted body of the train was my own
staring at the cut-up, patch-worked land, the first fence
not so tall as wide. In its wake, the final brush of tailwind
and the clacking sound of steel wheels against rails,
I could nearly hear the galloping hooves.

Pueblo

The fires of the sun
have already worked this world
till there is a sense of its dust
gritting into everything.

*

The pueblo glows red
in the sunset
like some immense heart.
You want to walk through
the chambers
with a broom
hoping to move
the dust into piles
—neat and unnatural.

*

While your own heart swings
like a porch lamp on a wire—
a beacon for the multifaceted eyes.
And somehow you build this
scene into an analogy of love.
Perhaps my own body begins
to twitch with the desire for light,
the false sun that rights the night earth.
Up or down,
I fall forward into the beams
of your heart
with a taste for flickering
and creaking wood
as unsure as I am
of what this body wants to be.

The Symbiotic Sunken City

Our city moves silently
towed by hovering fish
that look as clouds once did.

This metropolis is a jumble
of old facades held together
by straps and yellowing cement.

In the cold drowned daylight
someone is playing the blues
with a broken-string guitar—

but not sadly—only
in a shade of azure saved
for the deepest oceans.

The old women are gathering
nutrients in the currents breaking
around the foremost building.

Someone climbs the lines
with a scrub brush to keep
our savior fish clean.

We take our turns
at the daily chores, work
to keep the city in good graces.

In the evening, small prayers
are cast out into the eternal
silent abyss below us.

Everyone knows: god
is a fish, great banners of fins
stretching beyond our awareness.

And here, in this holy hour
of twilight, I too must confess—
to harboring dreams of swimming

on my own.

Prayer to the Peripheral

All afternoon the gods reveal themselves in animal clouds,
so one tribal legend is told, an oar in the water
of my mouth. Before any more secrets slip,
I have to genuflect in my creaking boat
an underbreath-prayer to the peripheral.
That fox god who remains the only muddy shore
for miles is listening to the underworld.
The hum of insects makes me
dizzy. A hungry biology I
sometimes forget
is mutual.
I pass right under the fox's muzzle,
my breath held
tight and small.

To Live in the Hair of the Sargasso Sea

You make use of the things stuck with you
—a pearl you cannot remember from where—
a faded relative from dry land
or impossible fable of an action figure.
You've made a lifetime of scraps
into a comfortable living space.
Ship planks you've always imagined
were once a Spanish galleon
framing the deep green twilit
mist. If not for the broken clock
and a pointless sundial,
you would not recall the notion of time.
An old captain's spyglass
reveals no ships off the port or bow.
New rips in the sail with its clear emblem
of futility. Another black fin
slices a narrow path through hair
you will neither steer to nor follow.
Approaching night and already the stars
call out to one another
like an oncoming downpour of toads.
The kettles and teapots are low of rain;
you have a vague notion of some song once chanted
that would split the sky into a downpour—
some other religion than your own.
Lightning flashing over the boiling triangle sea,
but it is as half-hearted as a torn map.
You might need to lie down for a spell
to work out what is needed
and what is written in the key of desire.
Another slow wave rolls under

and a lullaby voice is born.
Sleep comes with a green blanket of comfort:
everything has been provided for
by this god of static seas.

Every Dog is Two Dogs:

one that wags its tail waiting for my return
and one that has strewn my garbage through the house.
In my mind there are two dogs—both jump through
fiery hoops but one more willingly than the other.
Did I mention that both dogs are white? Yes, white
like the billowing fog that visits every afternoon.
One snaps and bites while barking loudly at the fog.
The other has run deep into the bank; except for the jingled
collar, it has become fog. It is a happy jingle.
I say this because the dog and the fog bobble my head.
So does the jingle. And the flaming hoops. My house.
And your ear. They are all in here. Do you hear
that? It is the *you* that I have imagined you to be
in a top hat running across the moors up to my door.
You say there is a telegram—one that I have imagined
you would always bring. It only reads *pastiche*.
And then we are in a European city of many architectures
even if you did not mean us to be. And the hoops have
set fire to these old buildings and the structures crumble
into flames and ruin like all European cities do. In the rubble
you say you hate the rhyming sounds. Everything should be
a beautiful symphony of tin pots and spoons. In the following
cacophony I wonder which mind I have imitated for you.
And the dogs are barking at each other. They are mad
that the one is not more like the other. They tug-of-war
your old sock—the one you wore while kicking dead horses.
You asked *why fiery hoops? Is this a circus?* I know you
hate this part. The doubt about whether you only exist
in someone else's mind. You reach into your top hat
for a rabbit but pull one of the white dogs by its ears—

it is not the happy hound. I fear for your hand, dear man.
Was that a haiku stamped on the brim of your hat? An old
Basho riff—imagine the world without frogs. Only dogs.
You unmagic your hat. Fold that telegram to a pocket square
for your tatty jacket. *I know, it's time to go*—you say
you hear the sound of circus tents pulled down. And both dogs
bark your departure—one grinning happy white razors;
the other straining to rip and steal your dusty blue soul.

Inlet

Slog through the creek
as the densities of gnarlwood
become mere ghosts
of themselves in the gloom.
I, too, feel a coming undone—
a separation of self from known
territories.
How many pinpoints of light
act like hope but are the small asses
of fireflies? I stumble upon
the damp fallen, snagged by
the bony grasp of their branches.
Feet numb with the cold current—
these things that trick and betray
me to stay, to give in, to take root
among the muddy banks as they do.
So I keep moving, lifting each
senseless foot up and forward.
Time is reinvented again—
another meaningless measure.
I've heard the odd birds call
to me like the voices of family
I'd all but learned to forget.
They beg: *come, come, why
did you ever leave us?* Before
my throat clears to answer,
they break into squabbling
caws, arguing over love's borders
as if I am a loosed seed
or nut. I do not stray. Upstream

I see much more of the same.
Fireflies where might be a sun.
Shale breaks itself into steps
rising away into the arms
of stranger trees. But I go on
listening to the babble-song
of water wearing down stone
and cutting into the land—
a slow blade. I walk the edge.
In some fantasy I harbor within
a hollow of my thicket soul,
I am the sun lighting the end
of this darkly lived tunnel.

Chronic

I shuffle the hallway between sleep and waking
as I lie in the twilight castoff of streetlamps.
I can feel the old house bones settling,
each creak a reminder of the damage
that occurs naturally over years
even as my own weights and pulleys strain
and groan with each turn into a new position.
Time, through rust and wear, has left
a wake of jagged edges.
Beyond my four walls the green world sighs,
wets itself down in preparation
and acceptance of things returning to soil—
the earth will take back everything,
regardless of whether the receipt is kept;
regardless of condition. In this way,
one can say the planet is forgiveness;
one could even say *love*—as a fine moss
envelops, becomes a shroud.
What I know about the world
is reduced to a garden of sharp points—
rugged rosettes prying at my vertebrae.
Sleep is unnecessary—the body's first lie.
This is often proclaimed at the point of drift
like the wet tying of a captain
to a ship's wheel as it pitches,
rolls creakingly to a choir—
sounds of lightning and splintering timbers.
The vessel is drawn to its own groundings.
Here the second lie is told:
what does not smash the boat
somehow becomes an improvement.

Walking the long hall back, I see the spines
of vipers, hear their hiss and protest
of my journey—another chorus of an epic tale
and the hero roughed-up and bruised,
returning to his waking life.

Aubade

...even more, I question the value of sunrises,

       the packaging of rosy fingers,

the wrapper more appealing to the lizard-eyed
consumer than what's within.

            From this vista

the sun looks a little bitter—
spiteful, and jealous—

       scorching the sky.

Mean ol' sun, looking down,
if I hang my head this morning,

     the back of my neck

will surely burn.

Mythos

A circle inherits a spiral;
the name *Fractal* is given

to a child. A cat curls into his
cradled arms and responds

only to *Schrödinger*.

Tightly in the gut of both,
dust swirls into the small

arms of galaxies. It is
a November twilight

and already the stars
are prepared for anything.

Considering the Minister of Eyes

what bothers me most is light seeping
into places not meant to be illuminated

the eyeball wants what the eyeball wants

now veins and arteries, bones, gristle
and nerve become pornography

wave after wave (and quantum mechanics
offers a new explanation with each)
a scientist leaves the room

the pot watched...
and Schrödinger's ghost laughs

nothing new under this or any star

sometimes when we hold hands
I see double helixes

what's wrong with you?

we run our animal smiles
right under each other's noses

and the eye remains unblinking
a window to the optic nerve of the observer soul

don't wrap me back up in flesh just yet

the clam of the mouth offers its low-tide opinion
but I feel the current anyway—electric
as though a storm is building
in the open sail of my skin

or is that just the tingling of my phantom limbs—
they still itch in my sleep

oh, it's all just the philosophy of floppy shadows

in my marrow I know there's a logical explanation
for every experience

but right now I don't want for reasons

I bathe in the bright slipstream of photons
gently messaging my lizard brain

Disturbance

A grave reopens as a bed
a bed with sheets of leaves

house of smoke and ash
house of mulch and autumn smoldering

one opens the window to let fog in
one watches at the sill as soot escapes

much of what has been built into the room
remains in gloom—frames of charcoal

a stump becomes a torso becomes
the last trick of low light

come to bed   is whispered repeatedly

night of insect love beneath a pillowed headstone
night of brambles

I tangle for you   comes out of the thick ether
the bed lies like an open cellar

she can willow her limbs, her fingers
in this exquisite limbo light

she takes on the curve and slant of her favorite font
she goes on quoting a favorite line from a movie

about the dead bee, only
out of context and darker than the original noire

momentarily the scattering light brightens
a yellow leaf or browning grass

aside from this no other color exists
on the monochrome palette

there is no black and white, only varying shades of gray
echoes from the dusty corners

followed by the undeniable rustle of movement—
an arm rising up, a hand opening

more twisting of bed sheets

what could have been love is not love
what has been love keeps its veil on

that image, that outline of her
looks down at the earthy bed

never scans the room

what is left of sound travels farther now
looking for its echo

the walls return to mist
and smoke

her name is spoken
—now the only disturbance

in the emptiness of the room

The Blue Hours

I wake you up in the age of horses
running a finger along your corral-gate latitudes.
When god ever speaks
it is with the voice of water—

Think *hurricane, tsunami.*

Then think *drop of rain.*

Here we are all shades of blue.
When we touch
there is an urge to twitch
our vestigial tails.

I never wish for explanations
nor reasons—

either believe
or live beneath an oppressive lens.

Raised by Coyotes

When we were together there was no desert,
no scrub brush, no urban sprawl.

At night, we went from house to house
looking for cracked windows and pet doors.

We thought ourselves a pack of wolves,
or at least that was always father's dream.

We would shuffle the pantry, tear into boxes,
dig out the plants from their pots.

Father would lie on the couch, the blue light
of television tiding over us.

Mice skittered and darted among the crumbs
of commercial breaks and station identifications.

Mother loved the taste of books—chewed page
after mysterious page.

I stayed under the coffee table, content
to close my eyes and listen to the dull banter

and the sitcom laugh-tracks and paint
the flickered scenes on my eyelids.

We were almost a pack once in the new western
desert of a tract home.

Song of the Brass Golem

First rain and I feel the rust
within my metal skin—

born to malformations
all those places on my body
where cooling cracked

and layers upon layers
of my flesh oddly fell
upon the bone.

I hear the cruel children
and their songs behind me
as I shuffle-step the hard walk

home. And though taunted
I have no room for hate
within the chambers

of my envious heart.
I slide the locks, draw
the curtains of the compartment

I call home, after another tedious
day as a doorstop.
Everyone has a purpose

and a place. So *they* say.
And *someone for everyone*
is often said, too. Though

I cannot imagine that
poor other soul, trapped
in her amalgam body.

A small prayer over candles
and my green dust breath
for no one else.

At night my father phones
with his pride and
commanding encouragements.

I eat brass tacks for dinner,
nodding before the TV drone,
and dream of becoming an idol,

young upon the screen—stage
lights gleaming
from my polished skin.

Faces of adoration, hands
reaching to touch
this life redeemed.

And each night in the fantasy
panel glow, I fashion
my mouth to sing.

Still Life with Suicide Bomber #1

Always this animated debate about the fruit
Eve pulled down from the Tree
of Knowledge. Others so certain

of pomegranates. And a few
who believe in how the shape of a pear fits
the human hand like a grenade. The shadow

of fruit with stems can be man-
ipulated into the rough horn of a devil.
Think of the ear as pear-shaped—

if only a human could hear like fruit does!
Imagine the music of pollination
each day, like a prayer-song;

that this is as close to God
as you will ever come. That the pluck
of a stem is not defilement

but a rebirth—a renewal of faith.
If mouths are as silent as pears
then seeds would be our common tongue.

I would speak my mind
in branches and leaves without fear
of another's terrible blossoming hand.

Still Life with Suicide Bomber #2

It is not that the world is a peach
although many disputes were settled
over peach wine. That fruit
sliced, sugared, and served
to a visiting tribe's emissary.
What is left is tactile: the peach
with its soft fuzz rubbing the finger-
tips. I used to think I could wear
my digits raw, repetition of a stroke

like its own kind of prophecy. But why
would anyone do this? Morbid teen
fascination? If I thought any longer
about my finger or the fruit
it would have turned into prayer.
I would have fantasized the raw
flesh stripped of its skin, the skeletal
spinnerets finger-pointing at god
every twilight. I would have said something
taught to be said. I would have touched
my chest and offered juice and bone,
blood and pit. I would have taken more
than was given to me.

Still Life with Suicide Bomber #3

O hand that appears to be asleep
and incapable
                        of its terrible blossom.
I prefer to think of cherries
stacked like cannonballs
but harmless,
                    red, not blood
                            red, like the release
of juice. Say *hangnail*, say *scarab*,
say *the earth is a flat square*.

                Believe the sea
is roiling with monsters and you are not
their distant relative. That we *too* are not related,
not a strand of DNA
nor common ancestor
standing upright
            for the first time—

say *Kane*, say *blastmark*,
                        say *blaspheme*—
                    repeat your justifications
                    like a lost prayer

        only you know the words to.
    Ours will be shared doom, but
blame everything on *God's will*.

O brother hand, I could have almost touched you
                        while you were asleep.

Still Life with Suicide Bomber #4

If I told you there were three gods in the sky,
each dying like a cut sunflower in a vase,

would you still search out a way to sacrifice
yourself on their behalf?

Even if they were shaking their heads not to?
Another petal falls from grace.

Their seedful centers look like a crowd
of black cloth-covered milling heads.

What if any of the gods just wanted fresh water?

What if the vase is merely painted
the color of blood?

Would you still need a cleric to suggest
a meaning? Or a priest to tell you

what was once said to be *good*? Someone
slices a pear to its seeds,

and the things most needed here
are soil and water.

Someone is asking God right now
for the strength to die with others.

If I told you there were three dying gods
like cut sunflowers

would you pray for clean water?

The Red Horse

I wore the night as my dress
and the wolf-boy flew his kite,

making use of our speed
as the red horse carried us

through the thinning trees
of Autumn. I held a dowsing

rod and thought it could lead me
to anything I needed, but the red

horse had its own course
which it led in full gallop.

I could see each bare branch,
gnarled and bony fingers. I

could see each blade of grass—
an imitation of golden-green fire.

I held the rein and the rod—
I thought that meant I could steer,

but the horse had its own course
and suddenly everything was clear.

I knew what the wolf-boy knew:
we were only along for the ride.

Calcium's Slender Embrace

Now I see that red means nothing
in this winter landscape
with flurries of snow
across the unfenced graveyard.

Don't stare at my ruby lips,
my love; color is wasted on the dead—
a mockery, a hush, a denial
of what the body has become.
I have no use for a dress
drenched in prismed memory.

Say "here lies" if you must.
Wish for one last impossible word
to sum a lifetime. Pretend you knew
me—I was always a field of wildflowers,
more than this patterned dress could ever say.
I was the roots and insects and the dew,
the wind-shaken stalks, the bones.

Now I have a new name for shadowed snow
that is more than the crunch and crackle,
a metered response for the end of life.
The slow grinding down, erosion. The entropy,
I know as *bone and ash scattered on frost*,

O calcium's slender embrace.
No fanfare for me. I am given to the whisper
wind and then back to the field
like seed. My voice
is the rasp of flake and dust,

the low thrum
of repeated soft impact,
so long in the field
it condenses to shell
the frozen ground.

This body no longer holds
my voice. I can never be written
or captured again. The words fall
and skitter like shrouds and veils
across the sparkled ice.
My name is no longer
my name.
I am calm.
I am moving
toward the promise
of Spring.

All That Remains

Once again the world is aflame
and all we have left is the priest

with his snuffed-out candle,
the picked-over bones

of our last meal, and the boy
of a mistake that I had prayed for

in his blue mask. The milk
and the tea are gone

like ashes and communion
wafers. The priest would

work fish and bread
if only we had some. I hold

my fork as though his prayer
and this gormless boy

might be a miracle in disguise—
a miracle that could

feed us all.

Souvenir

I was raised by hyenas and fire.
There was nothing that was mine; I served
the family—nursemaid, messenger, steward.
If they wanted something they snapped for it,
screaming at the entrance of their rooms.
(*That bone you have, that bone is mine.*)
No matter the outcome, I came
and scrubbed the blood out of the carpet,
then cleaned the wounds. I found a bone once,
dislodged in a fight—forgotten. I keep it
close to my breastbone, white and burning
the music of possession into my wit.

Acknowledgments

The author is grateful to the editors and staffs of the following magazines where these poems originally appeared, some in different versions: "Calcium's Slender Embrace," *At Length*; "Be That Releasable," *Bateau*; "A Little Night Music," *Blip*; "Disturbance," *Burning Bush2*; "Still Life With Suicide Bomber #3," *Cider Press Review*; "Frogpond," *Clade Song*; "Personal," *The Coachella Review*; "I, Michigan," "Urge Evolution," *diode*; "Piano from Scratch," *Driftwood Review*; "Nocturne," "Pueblo," "Mythos," "Inlet," *Forge*; "The Turning," *ForPoetry*; "Each Dog is Two Dogs," *FutureCycle Poetry*; "Prayer to the Peripheral," *Lily*; "Island," *Medulla Review*; "Magpie in My Own Image," *Memorious*; "The Blue Hours," "Aubade," *Milk Sugar*; "Song of the Brass Golem," *Mi Posia*; "Genesis in Retrograde," *Mississippi Review*; "Souvenir," "Invitation," "Legitimacy Is So Chummy," "Deadline World," "Magic, Isn't It," *The National Poetry Review*; "To Live in the Hair of Sargasso Sea," "Quadruple Life," *No Tell Motel*; "Raised by Coyotes," *OCHO*; "Aubade with Red Tail Hawk," *Off the Coast*; "All That Remains," *Pebble Lake Review*; "Knot," *Phren-Z*; "Blue Mountain at Sunset," "Martha's House of Cards," "El Amante," *Pirene's Fountain*; "Dispossessed," *Praxilla*; "Scarecrow," "Tempt" *Psychic Meatloaf*; "The Symbiotic Sunken City," *Nickel City Review*; "Unraveling Trees," "Persephone: Cream, Cherries, and the Diagramed Heart," "Considering the Ministry of Eyes," *radioactive moat*; "The Mirrored Narcissus," *Rufous City Review*; "We Form a Line," *Scapegoat Review*; "The Red Horse," *Shenandoah*; "[we lived on the crest of a wave]," *Sunrise from Blue Thunder: poems in response to the Japan earthquake and tsunami*; "The Listening Post," *Tiferet*; "Still Life With Suicide Bomber #1, #2, and #4," *Toad*; "Driven," *Weave*; "Landscape without Crossing Signal" *Willows Wept Review*

Cover art, "Still Life with an Eye," by AREPO (arepoproductions.com); cover and book design by Diane Kistner (dkistner@futurecycle.org); interior type, DejaVu Serif with Diavlo Bold titling

About FutureCycle Press

FutureCycle Press is dedicated to publishing lasting English-language poetry and flash fiction books, chapbooks, and anthologies in both print-on-demand and ebook formats. Founded in 2007 by long-time independent editor/publishers and partners Diane Kistner and Robert S. King, the press incorporated as a nonprofit in 2012. A number of our editors are distinguished poets and authors in their own right, and we have been actively involved in the small press movement going back to the early seventies.

Our annual anthology, *FutureCycle*, combines poetry and flash fiction. The FutureCycle Poetry Book Prize and honorarium is awarded annually for the best full-length volume of poetry we publish in a calendar year. We are dedicated to giving all authors we publish the care their work deserves, making our catalog of titles the most distinguished it can be, and paying forward any earnings to fund more great books.

We've learned a few things about independent publishing over the years. We've also evolved a unique, resilient publishing model that allows us to focus mainly on vetting and preserving for posterity the most books of exceptional quality without becoming overwhelmed with bookkeeping and mailing, fundraising activities, or taxing editorial and production "bubbles." To find out more about what we are doing, come see us at www.futurecycle.org.